People who he

Fire Service

Jillian Powell

HODDER
Wayland

an imprint of Hodder Children's Books

Contents

All Wayland books encourage children to read and help them improve their literacy.

✓ The page numbers and index can be used to locate a particular piece of information.

✓ The glossary reinforces alphabetic knowledge and extends vocabulary.

✓ The books to read section suggests other books dealing with the same subject.

Firefighters

Firefighters work in a team called a watch.

Firefighters are based at a fire station, where they practise fire fighting and rescue work. They are ready to answer **emergency calls** at any time.

The Control Centre

The people at the control centre answer emergency calls from people who need help.

When someone rings the **emergency services** to report a fire, a person at the control centre sends a message to the fire station nearest to the fire.

The firefighters leave the fire station as quickly as possible.

A fire bell rings to warn the firefighters that there is an emergency. They rush to the fire engine and jump in. They will put on helmets and special clothes.

The Fire Engine

The fire engine hurries to the fire.

The driver must drive quickly but safely. The team can talk to the control centre using a two-way radio.

The fire engine has warning sounds and lights.

Blue flashing lights warn other drivers to move out of the fire engine's way. A **siren** makes a loud noise so that drivers can hear the fire engine coming.

Firefighting

Firefighters need lots of water to put out fires.

A fire engine carries 1,800 litres of water. The firefighters can fix their **fire hoses** to **fire hydrants** in the road so that they can pump out more water.

Fires can happen in cars and lorries as well as buildings.

Cars and lorries can catch fire after an accident or if there is an **electrical fault**. The firefighters work quickly to put out the flames before the petrol tank blows up.

Rescue

Firefighters are trained to rescue people.

Firefighters use their ladders to reach tall buildings and rescue people who are injured or trapped by fire. They carry people to safety.

Firefighters sometimes need breathing masks.

Firefighters have to go inside smoky buildings to put out fires or rescue people. They wear breathing masks to protect them from the smoke.

Chemical Fires

Firefighters use foam to put out some fires.

Some fires cannot be put out with water. Firefighters use foam to put out fires when oil, petrol or **chemicals** are burning.

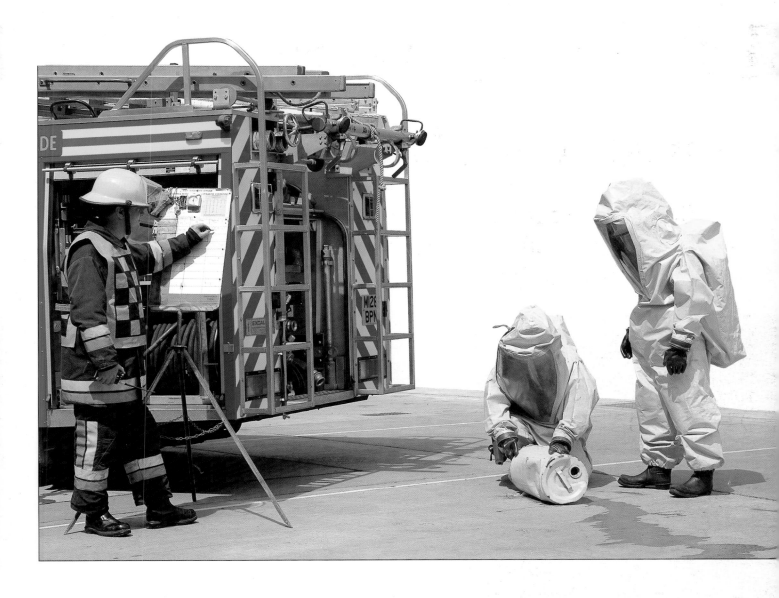

Firefighters wear special suits to protect them.

When chemicals burn, they can be poisonous.
Firefighters need to wear special **chemical
protection** suits.

Firefighters help when there has been a road accident.

Firefighters are trained to rescue people. If someone is trapped inside a car or lorry, the team uses special equipment to cut the person free.

Firefighters wash the road clean.

After an accident, there may be slippery oil or **diesel** on the road. The firefighters use a fire hose to wash the road. They make sure that no oil goes into the drains.

Floods

Firefighters help people and animals after a flood.

Heavy rain can make rivers overflow and flood people's homes. The fire service rescues people and animals from the floodwater.

The fire service uses rescue boats.

When the floodwater is deep, the fire service uses boats to reach people who are trapped in their homes.

Pumps are used to clear away water after floods.

Firefighters clear drains with rods and pumps so that the rain can run away. They also use pumps to pump out the floodwater from buildings.

Storm Damage

Firefighters make buildings safe after stormy weather.

Storms can damage buildings and make them dangerous. Very strong winds can blow down **scaffolding** and even walls. The fire service makes buildings safe.

Firefighters use special ladders to reach roofs.

Storms can blow away chimney pots and tiles from
house roofs. The fire service makes sure roofs are safe
and that the rain cannot get in.

Animal Rescue

Firefighters rescue animals that are trapped or in danger.

Firefighters use their ladders to reach cats that have become stuck in trees or on rooftops.

Animals on farms and in the countryside sometimes need help.

Firefighters use special equipment to rescue big animals such as cows or horses. They are using **lifting gear** to lift this horse out of a **swamp.**

Training

Firefighters practise using equipment at the fire station.

There is a tall tower at the fire station so firefighters can practise using ladders to rescue people from high buildings. The fire engine has controls that make the ladder go up and down.

Firefighters carry out rescue exercises.

Firefighters must know what to do in an emergency. They have training exercises so that they can practise rescuing people from accidents such as a rail crash.

Fire Safety

Fire investigators try to find out how a fire started.

Cooking accidents, electrical faults and cigarettes can all cause fires. Some fires are started on purpose by **arsonists**. The investigator looks for clues.

Displays show people how fires start.

Fire safety teams use special trucks to give displays on fire safety. They show people how fires can start in the home and how to put them out.

The Fire Station

The station officer inspects the watch.

Each watch is inspected every day to check that everyone is ready to start work.

Firefighters clean and check all the equipment.

The fire engines must always be ready to go out on emergency calls.

Firefighters tell schoolchildren about their work.

Sometimes firefighters can take a fire engine to visit a school.

Topic Web

ENGLISH
- Write instructions for fire safety
- Describe a fire

MATHS
- Make graphs to show how and where most fires start

SCIENCE
- Find out how fire changes different materials.
- Find out how we use fire for power

INFORMATION TECHNOLOGY
- Design a fire investigation report form

HISTORY
- Find out about the Great Fire of London
- Find out about the history of the Fire Service

Topic Web
FIRE SERVICE

GEOGRAPHY
- Make a fire escape plan
- Work out a route for the fire service

DESIGN AND TECHNOLOGY
- Design and make a firemark

ART
- Make fire paintings or collages

MUSIC
- Compose fire music

P.E.
- Perform a fire dance

Notes for Teachers

Fire and its properties provide an inspiring subject for designing, making and performing skills. Fire can be used to develop discursive and analytical skills through discussion of its good and useful properties, as well as its dangerous and destructive properties. National Fire Statistics showing how and where fires start give scope for applying mathematical skills.

Topics for Discussion

The work of the fire service provides a topic central to the idea of community and citizenship. It can be discussed in the context of other humanitarian services such as nursing, ambulance and lifeboat crews.

Although fire out of control can be destructive and dangerous, fire is also very useful and we cannot live without it. The information can be used to start a discussion on how we use fire, for cooking, heating and lighting, in power stations and for industry, as well as for celebration (bonfires, fireworks) and signalling.

The work of firefighters can be used in discussions on teamwork, and how individuals work within a team. Fire safety can be developed into a wider discussion of personal safety issues for the PSHE curriculum.

Topic Web Activities

ENGLISH
• Writing   • Speaking and listening
Pretend you are a fire prevention officer and write instructions for fire safety and a fire escape route for your home or school.
Imagine you have witnessed a fire being put out by the fire service. Write a description of what you saw.

MATHS
• Using and applying maths   • Handling data
Using recent National Fire Statistics, make a graph to show the main causes of fire in people's homes, e.g. cooking accidents, faulty wiring, heaters, cigarettes. Make another graph to show what caught fire, e.g. houses, chimneys, cars and lorries, woodland.

SCIENCE
• Experimental and investigative science
• Materials and their properties
Make a list of all the ways that fire is used by people. Find out how fire changes different materials, such as wood and wax. What happens when they are cooled again?

I.T.
• Communicating and handling information
Use the computer to design a fire report form that could be used to investigate how a fire started.

HISTORY
• Historical inquiry   • The Great Fire of London
• Victorian Britain   • The Second World War
Do a project about the Great Fire of London, using contemporary eye-witness accounts, paintings and other sources.
Find out when the fire service was established, and about its history.
Find out about the work of the fire service during air raids in the Second World War.

GEOGRAPHY
• Geographical skills
Make a plan for a fire escape route for your home. Find out about the fire escape routes at school.
Use a town plan to work out the quickest route from the fire station to the possible scene of a fire.

D.T.
• Designing and making skills
• Knowledge and understanding
Design and make a firemark for a building you know well (link with history). Mould it from plasticine or clay.

ART
• Investigating and making
Make fire pictures, using paint or collage to show the colour and patterns of flames.

MUSIC
• Performing and composing
Compose a piece of music using various instruments to make the sounds of fire and flames.

P.E.
• Dance
Choreograph and perform a dance around the theme of fire and flames.

Glossary

arsonists   People who set fire to buildings on purpose.

chemical protection   Special equipment to keep people safe from substances that can harm them.

chemicals   Substances that can be dangerous if not used carefully.

diesel   A type of fuel that burns in an engine.

electrical fault   When something that uses power goes wrong.

emergency calls   Urgent phone conversation to call out the fire service, police or ambulance services.

emergency services   Organizations that provide urgent help.

fire hoses   Long hoses that carry water to a fire.

fire hydrants   Water pipes in the street.

lifting gear   Special equipment for lifting heavy things.

scaffolding   A strong frame of metal poles for builders to stand on.

siren   A loud horn or bell.

swamp   Very wet land.

Books to Read

Cut-away Firefighters by Jon Kirkwood
(Watts/Aladdin, 1997)
A Day in the Life of a Firefighter by Carol Watson
(Watts, 1995)

Editors: Sarah Doughty and Cath Senker
Series editor: Sarah Doughty
Cover designer: Jan Sterling
Designer and typesetter: Malcolm Walker
Picture research: Gina Brown

First published in Great Britain in 1999
by Wayland (Publishers) Ltd

This edition published in 2001
by Hodder Wayland, an imprint of
Hodder Children's Books

Reprinted in 2002

© Hodder Wayland 1999

British Library Cataloguing in Publication Data
Powell, Jillian
  Fire Service. – (People who help us)
  1. Fire departments – Great Britain – Juvenile literature
  I. Title
363.3'0941

ISBN 0 7502 3491 1

Printed and bound by Grafiasa, Porto, Portugal

Index

Picture acknowledgements
Ace (Fotostock International) 12; Avon Fire Brigade 10, 17 (below), 18, 25; Eye Ubiquitous (Gary Trotter) 21; Firepix International (Tony Myers) 14 and 17 (above); Getty Images (Ben Edwards) 9; Robert Harding/Shout 4, 27 (above); Image Bank (Alan Becker) 7, (Steven Burr Williams) 20; Impact (Jeremy Nicholl) *title page*, (Sean Smith) 8, (Peter Arkell) 23; The Evesham Journal Series 16; Topham Picturepoint (Malcolm Croft) 15, (Adam Butler) 19, (John Giles) 24; Wayland Picture Library 3, 5, 6, 11, 13, 22, 26, 27 (below). Cover pictures: Firepix International/Tony Myers (main photo and top right); Wayland Picture Library (top left); Wayland/APM (top middle).